The StreetWise Guide to
BEING ENTERPRISING
WORKBOOK & JOURNAL

Increase Your Career, Business or Social Enterprise Prospects by using the E-Factor

David A. Gibson

Published by
OAK TREE PRESS
19 Rutland Street, Cork, Ireland
www.oaktreepress.com

© 2009 David A. Gibson

A catalogue record of this book is
available from the British Library.

ISBN 978 1 904887 33-1

All rights reserved.
No part of this publication may be reproduced or transmitted
in any form or by any means, including photocopying and
recording, without written permission of the publisher.
Such written permission must also be obtained before any part of
this publication is stored in a retrieval system of any nature.
Requests for permission should be directed to
Oak Tree Press, 19 Rutland Street, Cork, Ireland.

CONTENTS

	Introduction	5
1	The E-Factor Questionnaire	7
2	Your Strengths & Your Development Areas	12
3	Innovation & Creativity	14
4	Self-management	17
5	Negotiating the Deal	20
6	Personal Branding	23
7	Fear of Finance	26
8	Influence	29
9	Leadership & Teamwork	32
10	Action & Results	35
11	Your Personal Journal	38
12	90-day Review	84
	Notes	90
	About the Author	95
	About the StreetWise Guides	95

INTRODUCTION

This workbook is intended to be used in conjunction with **The Streetwise Guide to Being Enterprising** and it provides an opportunity for you to self-assess your level of enterprise skills, to tackle real-life problems, and to reflect on your results and adapt your behaviour, as appropriate. It includes activities to give you an opportunity to apply and to work on your enterprise skills, and to learn from the outcomes, since it is difficult to learn skills and behaviours from a book unless you practise and record the outcomes of activities where use the skill.

This workbook also provides a **Personal Journal** for you to record your daily activities and to reflect on what you have learned. There is a belief sometimes that people who are successful in life are born that way and, because they are successful, they don't make mistakes. However, research has shown that enterprising people "fail forward". What this means is that they look for opportunities to get involved in business and community activities, recognising that they will not always get things right the first time but that they will learn from each attempt and continue to learn and improve. No matter what degree of success you are experiencing, it is important to realise that we are all lifelong learners. Learn the lessons of life and, where possible, share them with other people.

The completed workbook not only provides a record of your own personal and business development, it is also very useful evidence for course tutors and business coaches to help them further your development and achievements.

If you are active in business and the community, there are lots of opportunities for you to get involved. You can acquire knowledge by reading but can only develop as a person if you take every opportunity to learn by doing things and by reflecting on what you have learned. The exciting thing about life, whether you are a student, a business leader or a retired pensioner, is that life offers a continual opportunity to learn. Take the opportunity to do this and your learning will have impact, not only on your own success but on helping others and making a contribution.

Start doing things. Start recording your learning. Start helping others with their development.

Professor David A Gibson
August 2009

Section 1
THE E-FACTOR QUESTIONNAIRE

Please rate yourself on a scale of 1 to 7 in terms of how frequently that you demonstrate the following behaviours (1 is **Almost Never**, 4 is **Generally**, and 7 is **Almost Always**). After you have completed the questionnaire, please add up and enter the sub-totals for each section. Then add up all the sub-section totals to produce your Grand Total on page 11.

1. INNOVATION & CREATIVITY—the ability to spot opportunities and challenges and to innovate continually.

1. Absorb and use new ideas and information quickly.	1	2	3	4	5	6	7
2. See the future with clarity	1	2	3	4	5	6	7
3. Find new ways to get better results from limited resources.	1	2	3	4	5	6	7
4. Good at judging which ideas to develop	1	2	3	4	5	6	7
5. Come up with a lot of new ideas and ways of working.	1	2	3	4	5	6	7
SUBTOTAL							

2. SELF-MANAGEMENT— the ability to master your own beliefs and emotions as a resource.

1. Recognise and learn from your mistakes.	1	2	3	4	5	6	7
2. Take criticism well.	1	2	3	4	5	6	7
3. Composed when taking risky decisions.	1	2	3	4	5	6	7
4. Make sound decisions quickly.	1	2	3	4	5	6	7
5. Seize opportunities.	1	2	3	4	5	6	7
SUBTOTAL							

3. NEGOTIATING THE DEAL— the ability to get the best deal for yourself and for your business.

1. Effective at countering objections to your proposals.	1	2	3	4	5	6	7
2. Prepared to say what you think.	1	2	3	4	5	6	7
3. Flexible and can change tack to win your way.	1	2	3	4	5	6	7
4. Have a good sense of timing.	1	2	3	4	5	6	7
5. Comfortable working alone against the odds.	1	2	3	4	5	6	7
SUBTOTAL							

4. PERSONAL BRANDING— the ability to market yourself and to research the market for maximum results.

1. Win people's attention by communicating a compelling message.	1	2	3	4	5	6	7
2. Make things happen for yourself.	1	2	3	4	5	6	7
3. Listen and take notice of what other people need and want.	1	2	3	4	5	6	7
4. Willing to ask for work.	1	2	3	4	5	6	7
5. Anticipate how you can meet other people's needs.	1	2	3	4	5	6	7
SUBTOTAL							

5. FINANCIAL ACUMEN—the ability to manage your financial affairs strategically to leverage the best returns.

1. Soundly evaluate the financial implications of a proposal.	1	2	3	4	5	6	7
2. Highly numerate.	1	2	3	4	5	6	7
3. Make realistic assumptions about the marketplace.	1	2	3	4	5	6	7
4. Constantly looking for better deals and returns.	1	2	3	4	5	6	7
5. Willing to take calculated risks.	1	2	3	4	5	6	7
SUBTOTAL							

6. INFLUENCE—the ability to influence events and others by selling and communicating.

1. Set your proposals in a wider business context.	1	2	3	4	5	6	7
2. Aware of rival products and competitors.	1	2	3	4	5	6	7
3. Act with customers in mind.	1	2	3	4	5	6	7
4. Good at sizing people up.	1	2	3	4	5	6	7
5. Gain support from others.	1	2	3	4	5	6	7
SUBTOTAL							

7. LEADERSHIP & TEAMWORK—the ability to lead teams and projects on a collaborative basis.

1. Involve others in almost all important decisions.	1	2	3	4	5	6	7
2. Build on other people's ideas.	1	2	3	4	5	6	7
3. Take responsibility for tough decisions.	1	2	3	4	5	6	7
4. Let people know where they stand.	1	2	3	4	5	6	7
5. Create a compelling picture of the future.	1	2	3	4	5	6	7
SUBTOTAL							

1: The E-Factor Questionnaire

8. ACTION & RESULTS— the ability to think strategically and to respond flexibly to feedback.

	1	2	3	4	5	6	7
1. Focus directly on what needs to be done.	1	2	3	4	5	6	7
2. Take risks that others would not attempt.	1	2	3	4	5	6	7
3. Persist when others would give up.	1	2	3	4	5	6	7
4. Push yourself and others for results.	1	2	3	4	5	6	7
5. Willing to bend (and break?) the rules to overcome obstacles.	1	2	3	4	5	6	7
SUBTOTAL							

YOUR E-FACTOR SCORE

1. INNOVATION & CREATIVITY	Sub-total	
2. SELF-MANAGEMENT	Sub-total	
3. NEGOTIATING THE DEAL	Sub-total	
4. PERSONAL BRANDING	Sub-total	
5. FEAR OF FINANCE	Sub-total	
6. INFLUENCE	Sub-total	
7. LEADERSHIP & TEAMWORK	Sub-total	
8. ACTION & RESULTS	Sub-total	
YOUR E-FACTOR GRAND TOTAL		

Section 2
YOUR STRENGTHS & YOUR DEVELOPMENT AREAS

What areas were you strong in?

What areas need development?

1: The E-Factor Questionnaire

What two key areas are you going to work on in the next 90 days?

What would you like to be able to do in 90 days?

ACTIVITY – YOUR PERSONAL JOURNAL

For the next 90 days, as you complete the exercises in the following sections, you are encouraged to monitor and reflect on your application and experience of your enterprise skills. In your **Personal Journal (Section 11)**, record which skills you have been practising that day.

Section 3
INNOVATION & CREATIVITY

An entrepreneurial person has the ability to identify opportunities for change and improvement. They are curious and capable of creating new ways of dealing with problems. They use their imagination, as well as their powers of analysis, to solve problems.

Sometimes, a problem can be solved simply by throwing more money at it. However, in many cases, an enterprising person has to find an innovative approach to solving a new problem with existing resources.

In your career, you will be called upon time and again to change things and to take projects forward. Solutions are not always obvious. The person who can combine different ideas and resources will make a significant impact.

ACTIVITY—INNOVATION & CREATIVITY

Active Ltd., a major consultancy firm focusing on the future, has appointed you as their new graduate trainee.

They want you to look at the problems of students in the UK and to come up with a list of ideas to put to their client, The Federation of UK Universities.

1. Brainstorm any problems you have had as a student.
2. Ask a random sample of 20 students to list problems they have had in their university careers.
3. With a small group of friends, take 20 minutes to list every possible solution to these problems.

3: Innovation & Creativity

Did you enjoy the task?

What worked well?

How could you have improved?

What have you learned from completing the task?

How will you use this skill in your everyday life?

Section 4
SELF-MANAGEMENT

Often, you will know what action you should take but fail to do so. Your toughest opponent will be yourself, your lack of motivation and ability to discipline yourself to take action to achieve your goals on a regular basis.

Learning to deal with your emotions to make the best use of time and to build your belief and self-confidence are all important.

Look for positive role models in people who seemed unlikely to succeed and yet believed in their abilities and ultimately succeeded.

It is important to know what motivates you and to use these motivating factors to take action. Most of you will respond to a crisis situation, but the successful entrepreneur will take action – for example, researching information at an early stage that will lead to success in the long term.

ACTIVITY – PERSONAL MASTERY

Find a recent project or task you had to complete but failed to do so.
1. Analyse why you did not manage to complete the task.
2. Whose fault was it?
3. How could you have motivated yourself to complete the task?
4. How could you have used your time more effectively?
5. What changes will you make to boost your future performance?

Did you enjoy the task?

What worked well?

How could you have improved?

4: Self-management

What have you learned from completing the task?

How will you use this skill in your everyday life?

Section 5
NEGOTIATING THE DEAL

Your business, career and life depend on the deals you make with friends, family and business associates.

People tend to get the deal they negotiate, rather than the deal they necessarily want or deserve. For instance, when visiting your bank manager to ask for a loan, you need to plan. How much do you want? What questions is the bank manager likely to ask? How will you approach the negotiation? Are you prepared to walk away if you don't get what you want?

A good negotiator prepares. He / she listens and understands the other person's position and attempts to reach a 'win - win' situation, where both parties gain something from the deal.

A good negotiator is flexible, patient and prepared to make offers and counter-offers to achieve the best possible deal.

ACTIVITY—NEGOTIATING THE DEAL

Look for a situation in your business / life / career where you feel you did not make a good deal.
1. Draw up a plan to set up a new negotiation
2. Do your homework: What do you want? What are the strengths and weaknesses of the person you are negotiating with? What are the awkward questions they might ask?
3. Go to the meeting, focus on listening and asking questions before you ask for anything. Try to remain calm and flexible. Try to enjoy the negotiation as a game.
4. How did you do? What did you learn from the negotiation?

5: Negotiating the Deal

Did you enjoy the task?

What worked well?

How could you have improved?

What have you learned from completing the task?

How will you use this skill in your everyday life?

Section 6
PERSONAL BRANDING

The concept of finding out what your customer wants and giving it to them profitably is just as important for an individual as for an organisation.

You may be starting a small personal services company or trying to establish a corporate career. In either case, knowing what the market wants and reaching that market, assuring them that you are the person with the solution, is vital.

Everything you do matters. You are a Brand and you need to engage in networking, public relations and promotion to ensure that everyone is aware of your capabilities.

Market yourself and your product or service to get the best possible results.

ACTIVITY – PERSONAL BRANDING

Your university has decided to set up an entrepreneurship society to promote enterprise and innovation to all students in your university. You have just signed a six-month contact as a part-time intern with responsibility to market the society to students and to make it a successful student society. You have a £1,000 budget.
1. How will you market the society?
2. Draw up an outline plan showing how you will use marketing concepts to establish the society.
3. How will you build both the society's and your own profile to ensure success?

Did you enjoy the task?

What worked well?

How could you have improved?

What have you learned from completing the task?

How will you use this skill in your everyday life?

Section 7
FEAR OF FINANCE

Money. It will play a significant part in your life. The ability to handle money, be profitable and make the right investments can create personal financial independence. However, even in not-for-profit organisations, just as much as in corporate projects, you will be expected to break-even and to make the best possible use of any funding source.

Too many entrepreneurial and corporate managers lack confidence in finance. Accountancy is simply a method of measuring business performance and keeping score.

Use your money resource to make the best financial performance and contribution for your organisation.

ACTIVITY – FEAR OF FINANCE

Your friend Daphne left university last year with a degree in communications and, since then, she has been running a PR agency. She is very busy and successful but she seems very stressed. She asks for your help as she knows you are developing your financial skills.

"I have no idea how I am doing. To keep up the appearance of doing well, I am driving a Mercedes, costing me £400 per month and I rent an apartment in the West End at £1,500 per month. I am getting lots of work but my bank manager is turning nasty and my Cashpoint card won't work".

You look her financial records and find that Daphne has sales of £50,000 for nine months trading and that her business expenses are £35,000. She is owed £10,000 and is three months behind on her car payments. How is she doing?

Use your financial skills to turn things around.

7: Fear of Finance

Did you enjoy the task?

What worked well?

How could you have improved?

What have you learned from completing the task?

How will you use this skill in your everyday life?

Section 8
INFLUENCE

It would be nice to say that the people with the most intelligence, who get the best degrees, have the most successful careers.

However, one of the key skills of the enterprising graduate is the ability to persuade potential employers to offer you a job, or a potential customer to buy your product or service. This process is helped by having a network of key people who will help you get the chance to 'make your pitch'.

The ability to persuade others to back you financially or to buy from you is the key to getting results in business.

Build your contact-base and continually practice your influencing skills in real-life situations. Listen to others and show them how you can meet their needs and expectations.

"Ask for the sale".

ACTIVITY – PERSONAL INFLUENCE

1. Come up with an idea for a product or service that will benefit a local charity.
2. Arrange a meting with the local manager of the charity and attempt to persuade him / her to introduce your idea to raise funds for the charity.
3. Once your have done this, arrange three meetings with local businesses with a profile for sponsoring charity products / services.
4. Your goal is to get their involvement in sponsoring the provision of the product / service.

Did you enjoy the task?

What worked well?

How could you have improved?

8: Influence

What have you learned from completing the task?

How will you use this skill in your everyday life?

Section 9
LEADERSHIP & TEAMWORK

Your ability to work as a part of a team will influence your business and your career progress. Unlike university, you often will have to work in a variety of teams, often with people from different backgrounds or culture, or level of skills. You may have to work with others with whom you find difficulty in building rapport.

It is important that you investigate your particular ways of working and what you can bring to the team.

Equally, you may need to lead a team. In certain instances, you may need to facilitate a team to achieve the team objectives. A team-player who leads may seem to be a paradox. However, leadership is much more than being a team-player – as an enterprising person you need to lead the team and to facilitate the team to meet its objectives.

ACTIVITY – LEADERSHIP & TEAMWORK

1. Identify a project or event that you want to make happen.
2. Get a small group of friends involved.
3. Assign roles and give everyone a chance to be a leader of the project.
4. Keep a record of each stage of the group's progress.
5. Ask the team members to keep a record also.
6. When you have completed the project, compare notes.

What leadership style worked best?
Did the team work or not?

Did you enjoy the task?

What worked well?

How could you have improved?

What have you learned from completing the task?

How will you use this skill in your everyday life?

Section 10
ACTION & RESULTS

Many business people / entrepreneurs seem to fit into two categories: some think ahead, plan strategically and make detailed business plans that never come to fruition, whereas others run around 'like headless chickens' doing things in a chaotic fashion that is more likely to set the organisation back than take it forward.
   Which are you?
   Which type should you be?
   The answer, of course, is that outcome planning and action orientation are both needed in business and social enterprise.
   Before action is taken, the enterprising manager / entrepreneur must be clear about their goals. Then, and only then, is it time to take action, review results and, if necessary, refine and modify strategy until the goal is reached.
   "Finding balance is the key".

ACTIVITY – ACTION & RESULTS
Create an outline plan showing where you want your career or business to be in five years' time.
Identify the action steps needed to take you there.
Draw a timeline for these activities.
Create a weekly action plan to kick-start your career / business.
Do two things on that action plan now before leaving this section.

Did you enjoy the task?

What worked well?

How could you have improved?

10: Action & Results

What have you learned from completing the task?

How will you use this skill in your everyday life?

Section 11
YOUR PERSONAL JOURNAL

For the next 90 days, as you complete the exercises in this **Workbook**, you are encouraged to monitor and reflect on your application and experience of your enterprise skills by completing a **Personal Journal**, where you can record which skills you have been doing that day.

Use this structure:
1. What worked—and why?
2. What didn't work—and why?
3. What will you do differently tomorrow?
4. What have you learned about yourself / your skills?

Your name: _____

Class / Group: _____

Journal start date: _____

11: Your Personal Journal

Day 1   **Date:** _____

Day 2   **Date:** _____

Day 3　Date: _____

Day 4　Date: _____

11: Your Personal Journal 41

Day 5   **Date:** _____

Day 6   **Date:** _____

Day 7   **Date:** _____

Day 8   **Date:** _____

Day 9 Date: _____

Day 10 Date: _____

Day 11   Date: _____

Day 12   Date: _____

Day 13   **Date:** _____

Day 14   **Date:** _____

Day 15   Date: _____

Day 16   Date: _____

Day 17   Date: _____

Day 18   Date: _____

Day 19 Date: _____

Day 20 Date: _____

Day 21   Date: _____

Day 22   Date: _____

Day 23 Date: _____

Day 24 Date: _____

Day 25 Date: _____

Day 26 Date: _____

Day 27   Date: _____

Day 28   Date: _____

Day 29 Date: _____

Day 30 Date: _____

Day 31 Date: _____

Day 32 Date: _____

Day 33 Date: _____

Day 34 Date: _____

Day 35 Date: _____

Day 36 Date: _____

Day 37   Date: _____

Day 38   Date: _____

Day 39   **Date:** _____

Day 40   **Date:** _____

11: Your Personal Journal

Day 41 **Date:** _____

Day 42 **Date:** _____

Day 43   Date: _____

Day 44   Date: _____

Day 45 Date: _____

Day 46 Date: _____

Day 47   Date: _____

Day 48   Date: _____

Day 49 Date: _____

Day 50 Date: _____

Day 51 Date: _____

Day 52 Date: _____

11: Your Personal Journal

Day 53   **Date:** _____

Day 54   **Date:** _____

Day 55   Date: _____

Day 56   Date: _____

Day 57   Date: _____

Day 58   Date: _____

Day 59   Date: _____

Day 60   Date: _____

11: Your Personal Journal

Day 61 **Date:** _____

Day 62 **Date:** _____

Day 63 **Date:** _____

Day 64 **Date:** _____

Day 65   Date: _____

Day 66   Date: _____

Day 67   Date: _____

Day 68   Date: _____

Day 69 **Date:** _____

Day 70 **Date:** _____

Day 71   Date: _____

Day 72   Date: _____

Day 73   Date: _____

Day 74   Date: _____

Day 75   Date: _____

Day 76   Date: _____

11: Your Personal Journal

Day 77　　**Date:** _____

Day 78　　**Date:** _____

Day 79   Date: _____

Day 80   Date: _____

Day 81   **Date:** _____

Day 82   **Date:** _____

Day 83   Date: _____

Day 84   Date: _____

Day 85   Date: _____

Day 86   Date: _____

Day 87   **Date:** _____

Day 88   **Date:** _____

11: Your Personal Journal

Day 89   **Date:** _____

Day 90   **Date:** _____

Section 12
90-DAY REVIEW

You have now completed the 90-day plan. Review your **Personal Journal** and then re-take the E-Factor self-assessment questionnaire on the following pages.

Are your scores any different from the questionnaire you completed when you started this workbook, 90 days ago?

What have you learned?

What are your next steps?

You now know how to change your strategies to achieve success—now is the time for you to just do it!

Throughout your career, you will never stop learning, so I encourage you to enjoy the process.

Congratulations on your achievement but, remember, you can always continue to improve!

Good Luck! And may your E-Factor always shine bright!

David A. Gibson

1. INNOVATION & CREATIVITY—the ability to spot opportunities and challenges and to innovate continually.

1. Absorb and use new ideas and information quickly.	1	2	3	4	5	6	7
2. See the future with clarity.	1	2	3	4	5	6	7
3. Find new ways to get better results from limited resources.	1	2	3	4	5	6	7
4. Good at judging which ideas to develop.	1	2	3	4	5	6	7
5. Come up with a lot of new ideas and ways of working.	1	2	3	4	5	6	7
SUBTOTAL							

2. SELF-MANAGEMENT— the ability to master your own beliefs and emotions as a resource

1. Recognise and learn from your mistakes.	1	2	3	4	5	6	7
2. Take criticism well.	1	2	3	4	5	6	7
3. Composed when taking risky decisions.	1	2	3	4	5	6	7
4. Make sound decisions quickly.	1	2	3	4	5	6	7
5. Seize opportunities.	1	2	3	4	5	6	7
SUBTOTAL							

3. NEGOTIATING THE DEAL— the ability to get the best deal for yourself and for your business.

1. Effective at countering objection to your proposals.	1	2	3	4	5	6	7
2. Prepared to say what you think.	1	2	3	4	5	6	7
3. Flexible and can change tack to win your way.	1	2	3	4	5	6	7
4. Have a good sense of timing.	1	2	3	4	5	6	7
5. Comfortable working alone against the odds.	1	2	3	4	5	6	7
SUBTOTAL							

4. PERSONAL BRANDING— the ability to market yourself and to research the market for maximum results.

1. Win people's attention by communicating a compelling message.	1	2	3	4	5	6	7
2. Make things happen for yourself.	1	2	3	4	5	6	7
3. Listen and take notice of what other people need and want.	1	2	3	4	5	6	7
4. Willing to ask for work.	1	2	3	4	5	6	7
5. Anticipate how you can meet other people's needs.	1	2	3	4	5	6	7
SUBTOTAL							

5. FINANCIAL ACUMEN—the ability to manage your financial affairs strategically to leverage the best returns.

1. Soundly evaluate the financial implications of a proposal.	1	2	3	4	5	6	7
2. Highly numerate.	1	2	3	4	5	6	7
3. Make realistic assumptions about the marketplace.	1	2	3	4	5	6	7
4. Constantly looking for better deals and returns.	1	2	3	4	5	6	7
5. Willing to take calculated risks.	1	2	3	4	5	6	7
SUBTOTAL							

6. INFLUENCE—the ability to influence events and others by selling and communicating.

1. Set your proposals in the wider business context.	1	2	3	4	5	6	7
2. Aware of rival products and competitors.	1	2	3	4	5	6	7
3. Act with customers in mind.	1	2	3	4	5	6	7
4. Good at sizing people up.	1	2	3	4	5	6	7
5. Gain support from others.	1	2	3	4	5	6	7
SUBTOTAL							

7. LEADERSHIP & TEAMWORK – the ability to lead teams and projects on a collaborative basis.

1. Involve others in almost all important decisions.	1	2	3	4	5	6	7
2. Build on other people's ideas.	1	2	3	4	5	6	7
3. Take responsibility for tough decisions.	1	2	3	4	5	6	7
4. Let people know where they stand.	1	2	3	4	5	6	7
5. Create a compelling picture of the future.	1	2	3	4	5	6	7
SUBTOTAL							

8. ACTION & RESULTS— the ability to think strategically and to respond flexibly to feedback.

1. Focus directly on what needs to be done.	1	2	3	4	5	6	7
2. Take risks that others would not attempt.	1	2	3	4	5	6	7
3. Persist when others would give up.	1	2	3	4	5	6	7
4. Push your self and others for results.	1	2	3	4	5	6	7
5. Willing to bend (and break?) the rules to overcome obstacles.	1	2	3	4	5	6	7
SUBTOTAL							

YOUR E-FACTOR SCORE, 90 DAYS LATER

1. INNOVATION & CREATIVITY	Sub-total	
2. SELF-MANAGEMENT	Sub-total	
3. NEGOTIATING THE DEAL	Sub-total	
4. PERSONAL BRANDING	Sub-total	
5. FEAR OF FINANCE	Sub-total	
6. INFLUENCE	Sub-total	
7. LEADERSHIP & TEAMWORK	Sub-total	
8. ACTION & RESULTS	Sub-total	
YOUR E-FACTOR GRAND TOTAL		

NOTES

NOTES

NOTES

NOTES

NOTES

OAK TREE PRESS
is Ireland's leading business book publisher.

It develops and delivers
information, advice and resources
to entrepreneurs and managers –
and those who educate and support them.

Its print, software and web materials are in use in Ireland, the UK, Finland, Greece, Norway, Slovenia, India, Pakistan and Sri Lanka.

OAK TREE PRESS
19 Rutland Street
Cork, Ireland
T: + 353 21 4313855
F: + 353 21 4313496
E: info@oaktreepress.com
W: www.oaktreepress.com

About the Author

David A. Gibson is a law graduate and a chartered accountant. He is a senior lecturer in Enterprise at Queen's University, Belfast. He is also an entrepreneur, who has owned and led several enterprises. He is passionate about developing an enterprise culture and provides advice and support for start-up businesses (both private and social enterprise). His belief that enterprise skills can be taught has spilled over into other areas of outreach, including the public sector. He also works as a financial consultant, developing exit strategies for family-owned enterprises.

About the StreetWise Guides

You can find out more about the **StreetWise Guides** series at **www.streetwisecentral.com**.